W9-AAE-231

Technology of Ancient Rome

Daniel C. Gedacht

The Rosen Publishing Group's
PowerKids Press™
PRIMARY SOURCE
New York

For the Magnificent Seven: Alex, Mary, Xandy, Caity, Lindsay, Andrew, and Ryan

Published in 2004 by The Rosen Publishing Group, Inc.
29 East 21st Street, New York, NY 10010

First Edition

Editor: Rachel O'Connor
Book Design: Michael J. Caroleo
Photo Researcher: Adriana Skura

Photo Credits: Cover © Royalty-Free/CORBIS; cover (inset), p. 16 (top) © Erich Lessing/Art Resource, NY; p. 4 © Fototeca International Lda/Art Resource, NY; p. 4 (map) The Granger Collection, New York; pp. 7, 8, 16 (bottom), 19 (top), 20 © Scala/Art Resource, NY; p. 11 (top) © Andrew Brown, Ecoscene/CORBIS; p. 11 (bottom) © Rugerro Vani/CORBIS; p. 12 © SEF/Art Resource, NY; p. 15 The Art Archive; p. 19 (bottom) Gilles Mermet/Art Resource, NY.

Gedacht, Daniel C.
Technology of ancient Rome / Daniel C. Gedacht.— 1st ed.
    p. cm.—(Primary sources of ancient civilizations. Rome)
Includes bibliographical references and index.
Contents: Technology helps build cities—Tools of technology—Roman homes—Aqueducts—Roman highways—Military technology—Roman ships—The Roman calendar—Medicine—Astronomy and mathematics.
  ISBN 0-8239-6779-4 (library binding)—ISBN 0-8239-8947-X (paperback)
1. Technology—Rome—History—Juvenile literature. 2. Rome—History—Juvenile literature. [1. Technology—Rome—History. 2. Rome—History.] I. Title. II. Series.
  T16.G43 2004
  609.37—dc21
                                                                    2003002791

Manufactured in the United States of America

Contents

Technology Helps Build Cities   5

Tools of Technology   6

Heating Technology   9

Aqueducts   10

Roman Highways   13

Military Technology   14

Roman Ships   17

The Roman Calendar   18

Medicine   21

Astronomy   22

Glossary   23

Index   24

Primary Sources   24

Web Sites   24

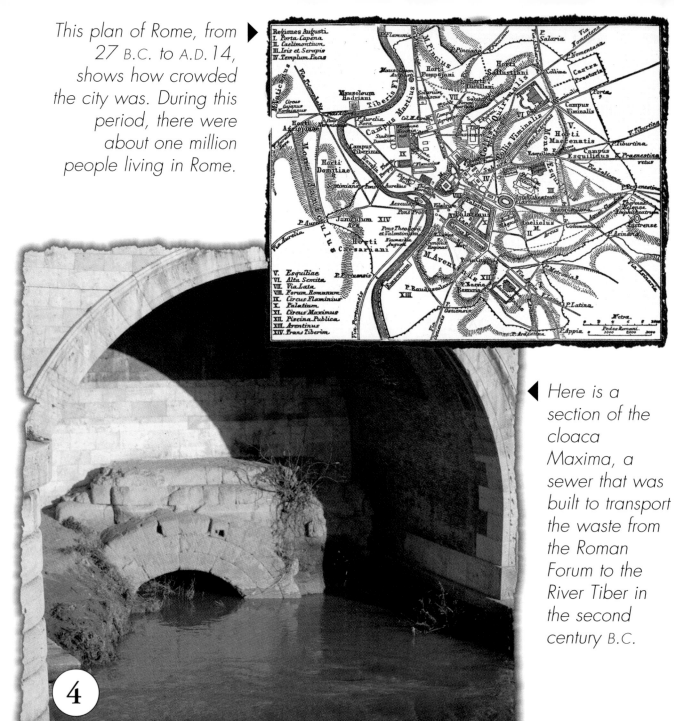

This plan of Rome, from 27 B.C. to A.D. 14, shows how crowded the city was. During this period, there were about one million people living in Rome.

Regiones Augusti.
I. Porta Capena.
II. Caelimontium.
III. Isis et Serapis.
IV. Templum Pacis.
V. Esquiliae
VI. Alta Semita.
VII. Via Lata.
VIII. Forum Romanum.
IX. Circus Flaminius.
X. Palatium.
XI. Circus Maximus.
XII. Piscina Publica.
XIII. Aventinus.
XIV. Trans Tiberim.

Here is a section of the cloaca Maxima, a sewer that was built to transport the waste from the Roman Forum to the River Tiber in the second century B.C.

4

Technology Helps Build Cities

By the first century A.D., Rome had become the biggest and most advanced city in the world. The ancient Romans came up with new technologies to improve the city's sanitation systems, roads, and buildings. They developed a system of aqueducts that piped freshwater into the city, and they built sewers that removed the city's waste.

The wealthiest Romans lived in large houses with gardens. Most of the population, however, lived in apartment buildings made of stone, concrete, or limestone. The Romans developed new techniques and used materials such as volcanic soil from Pozzuoli, a village near Naples, to make their cement harder and stronger. This concrete allowed them to build large apartment buildings called *insulae*.

5

Tools of Technology

Metal was important to Roman technology. Using metal, the Romans were able to make coins, pots, and pans. They also used metal in architecture. Metal became more important as Rome's power grew. More soldiers meant that more iron, copper, and bronze were needed to make swords and armor. The Roman army discovered large mines of copper and iron, along with some of gold and silver, in northern Africa and Spain. Romans mined the metals by either digging tunnels into the ground or digging up the earth and sifting through it for valuable materials. After metals were taken from the ground, they were heated and shaped into weapons, farming tools, and household goods.

Romans used metal to make objects such as this bronze carriage, or wheeled object used to carry people. ▼

Romans also used metal to make a soldier's swords and breastplate, as shown here. ▲

Heating Technology

Around the first century B.C., Romans created a new technology for heating homes, called hypocaust. It worked by allowing heat to travel under floors and through open spaces or pipes in the walls. Roman builders laid the floor of concrete blocks on tiles about 2 feet (.6 m) high. They built a furnace underneath the floor at one end of the house. As the fire burned, suction in the walls' open spaces dragged the heat and smoke upward and throughout the house. A big fire would create too much smoke, so someone had to keep a small fire of twigs and sticks burning continuously. The hypocaust kept homes warm but often made them stuffy and smoky.

◀ *In these ruins of an ancient Roman home, you can see the heating pipes that were built within the walls of the house.*

Aqueducts

The Roman government provided the people in the city with enough clean water for cooking and washing. In early Rome, water from the Tiber River was sufficient. As Rome's population grew, however, this water became dirty and polluted.

The Romans built aqueducts to transport clean water into the city from sources outside. Aqueducts were channels made of brick or stone and lined with concrete. The Romans built most of the aqueducts under the ground, but some ran above ground. These sections sat on raised, arched bridges called arcades. By the third century A.D., there were 11 aqueducts that carried around 300 million gallons (1.1 billion l) of water into the city every day.

Aqueducts carried water from the sources to large water tanks in the city. Above: This is a Roman aqueduct in Nerja, Spain. Left: Here is the Claudian Aqueduct near Rome.

Roman Highways

Rome was able to spread its empire partly because the Romans used technology to build large and effective systems of roads. The Romans planned and built highways that directly connected Rome with the territories that it conquered. This allowed soldiers and traders to travel quickly throughout the empire. In 312 B.C., the Romans built the first improved road, the Via Appia. Dirt roads had existed before, but the new roads were sturdier. The Romans built the new roads in layers. The first layer consisted of soil and stone. The next layer was often material such as sand and gravel mixed with clay. The surface layer was made of gravel or large pieces of stone.

Here is the Via Appia, or the Appian Way, as it looks today. The fact that the road still remains shows how strong the Roman roads were. The ancient Romans built more than 50,000 miles (80,467.2 km) of road.

13

Military Technology

Rome was often at war, either defending or expanding its empire. Roman soldiers used some of the same weapons the Greeks and Etruscans had used before them, such as catapults. The Romans, however, also developed new and improved weapons. This made their army more efficient and powerful. They made 5-foot (1.5-m) wooden poles, called pilums, with metal points. Soldiers on foot could jab their enemies with these poles. The Romans also made a small sword from metal, called a *gladius*, which was light and easier to thrust than a long, heavy one. They also made weapons that could kill enemies from a distance, such as crossbows, or *scorpios*.

This sculpture is from the Arch of Constantine, which was built in A.D. 315. It shows Roman soldiers in battle, armed with shields and weapons. ▶

15

▲ *Romans needed to bring in grains and other agricultural products from their territories in North Africa, Spain, and Turkey. While traders carried some items over land on the highways, most transported their goods by ship.*

Roman Ships

Rome extended its territory around the Mediterranean Sea. It was faster and easier to trade goods with some areas by sea. The Romans made their ships from wood. Some ships, especially the larger ones, had metal supports attached to the smooth surface to strengthen the sides. Sea winds were changeable, so rowers with oars powered most boats. However, some boats had square sails to take advantage of winds when they came. These boats were important for bringing supplies to Rome from its territories around the Mediterranean. Merchant ships were usually from 100 to 130 feet (30.5–39.6 m) long and carried up to 550 tons (499 t) of supplies.

The Romans built ships to transport their armies. This sculpture shows a Roman warship that appears on the Temple of Fortuna Primigenia.

The Roman Calendar

Early Romans developed a calendar so that they could keep track of the agricultural seasons and religious holidays. This early calendar had 10 months. Because it was different than the actual solar year, the farming seasons did not occur during the same months every year. At the request of Julius Caesar, Rome's leader, astronomers worked to fix this problem. In 46 B.C., the calendar was changed to give the year 365 days. The Julian calendar, as it is called, is the basis for our calendar today. Its year was divided into 12 months, its week was seven days, and one day lasted 24 hours. Roman farmers could now better organize their planting and harvesting times.

This illustrated calendar shows the seasons and the months. Months and days in the Roman calendar were named for the planets and Roman gods, such as Janus, the god of beginnings, for January. ▶

This is a piece from a Roman calendar that can be seen in the National Museum in Italy. ▶

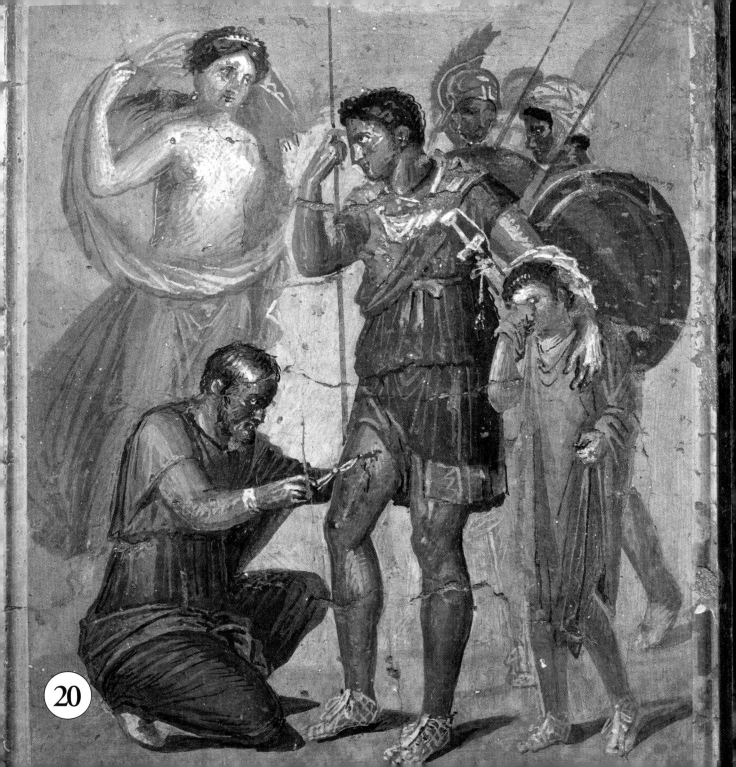

Medicine

Health care in early Roman times was very basic and relied on religion. Anyone could claim to be a doctor, because no qualifications were needed. In addition to prayer or sacrifice to the gods, Roman doctors used such things as blood, crushed insects, and plants to treat patients. Much of this was worthless, and the Romans had little defense against illnesses such as smallpox and tuberculosis, which killed thousands of people.

In the second century A.D., when the Roman Empire included lands such as Egypt and Greece, a Greek doctor and scientist called Galen moved to Rome. Galen made great advances in medical studies, particularly in areas such as the lungs and the heart.

◄ *In this Roman painting, a doctor is shown attending to the wounds of Aeneas, the hero of Virgil's poem the* Aeneid.

Astronomy

Ancient Romans studied astronomy to understand the universe and the planets. Astronomy helped them to make maps and create their calendar. A Greek man called Ptolemy was among the most famous astronomers in the Roman Empire. Ptolemy believed that Earth was the center of the universe and all the other planets and the Sun circled around it. This belief held until the sixteenth century A.D.

The ancient Romans brought new technologies to people throughout the empire. The advances that the Romans made in science, military techniques, architecture, and construction materials were among the reasons why the Roman Empire was so powerful for so many centuries.

Glossary

architecture (AR-kih-tek-cher) Designing and making buildings.

astronomers (uh-STRAH-nuh-merz) People who study the Sun, the Moon, the planets, and the stars.

catapults (KA-tuh-pults) Ancient weapons, which worked like huge slingshots, for throwing huge rocks at the enemy.

concrete (KON-kreet) A hard, strong building material made by mixing water, rocks, and gravel with a binding element.

crossbows (KROS-bohz) Weapons used in the Middle Ages that consisted of bows mounted across wooden blocks.

developed (dih-VEH-lupt) Worked out in great detail.

materials (muh-TEER-ee-uls) What things are made of.

mines (MYNZ) Underground tunnels from which stones are taken.

sanitation (sa-nih-TAY-shun) Getting rid of trash and human waste.

sewers (SOO-erz) Underground pipes that carry waste.

smallpox (SMOL-poks) A serious and often fatal sickness that causes a rash and leaves marks on the skin.

solar year (SOH-ler YEER) Relating to the 365 days it takes for the Earth to travel around the Sun.

suction (SUK-shun) The process of drawing liquids or gases into space by sucking out part of the air from that space.

techniques (tek-NEEKS) Ways of doing something.

transport (TRANZ-port) Move something from one place to another.

tuberculosis (too-ber-kyuh-LOH-sis) A sickness that affects the lungs.

Index

A
aqueducts, 5, 10
arcades, 10
astronomy, 22

C
calendar, 18

I
illnesses, 21
insulae, 5

G
gladius, 14

H
hypocaust, 9

M
maps, 22
Mediterranean Sea, 17

P
pilums, 14
Ptolemy, 22

R
roads, 5, 13

S
sanitation, 5
ships, 17
soldiers, 6, 14

W
weapons, 6, 14

Primary Sources

Cover. Pont du Gard Aqueduct. Nimes, France. The tiered-arch structure spans the Gard River, rising to 160 feet (49 m) above the water. **Inset.** Bronze shovel. First to third centuries A.D. Musee des Antiquites Nationales, France. **Page 4. Top.** Plan of Rome. 27 B.C.–A.D. 14. **Bottom.** Tiber river outlet, water conduit. **Page 7. Right.** Breastplate and swords of a Roman centurion. Second century A.D. Museo della Civilta Romano. **Page 8.** The remains of heating pipes in the Casa del Triclinio. **Page 11. Top.** Roman aqueduct. Nerja, Spain. Photograph by Andrew Brown, circa 1970–1994. **Bottom.** The Claudian Aqueduct. Campagna Romana, Rome, Italy. Photograph by Ruggero Vanni. **Page 15.** Roman stone relief from the Arch of Constantine, shows soldiers and legionaries in battle. A.D. 315. The arch was erected in honor of Emperor Constantine after the battle in which he defeated Maxentius at the Milvian Bridge. **Page 16. Top.** Two ships sailing against waves. A man is overboard. Marble relief from a Roman sarcophagus. Second to third centuries A.D. **Bottom.** War ship from the Temple of Fortuna Primigenia, at Praeneste, Italy. First century A.D. **Page 19.** Illustrated calendar of the seasons and the months. Mosaic from the first half of the second century A.D. **Page 20.** A doctor attends to the wounds of Aeneas. Roman fresco. First to third centuries A.D.

Web Sites

Due to the changing nature of Internet links, PowerKids Press has developed an online list of Web sites related to the subject of this book. This site is updated regularly. Please use this link to access the list:
www.powerkidslinks.com/psaciv/techrom/